MW00709542

Hydroponics for

Beginners

The Ultimate DIY guide to Start Growing Herbs, Fruits and Vegetables at Home Without Soil. Build A Perfect and Inexpensive Hydroponic Growing Gardening System

Copyright © 2020 [Nick Brown]

Legal & Disclaimer

The information contained in this book and its contents is not designed to replace or take the place of any form of medical or professional advice; and is not meant to replace the need for independent medical, financial, legal or other professional advice or services, as may be required. The content and information in this book have been provided for educational and entertainment purposes only.

The content and information contained in this book have been compiled from sources deemed reliable, and it is accurate to the best of the Author's knowledge, information, and belief. However, the author cannot guarantee its accuracy and validity and cannot be held liable for any errors and/or omissions. Further, changes are periodically made to this book as and when needed. Where appropriate and/or necessary, you must consult a professional (including but not limited to your doctor, attorney, financial advisor or such other professional advisor) before using any of the suggested remedies, techniques, or information in this book.

Table of Contents

WHAT IS HYDROPONIC?..11

HYDROPONICS..18

Why do plants increased using hydroponics grow faster than plants which do not put it to use? 18

How hard will it be to use hydroponics equipment? 19

HYDROPONIC GARDENING SYSTEM 20

A concise history of hydroponics 20

Are there really benefits to using hydroponics?...................21

Hydroponic systems..21

You want to purchase or make a method your self..............22

Which exactly are hydroponic grow tents?...........................22

Exactly what exactly are they? 23

Just how can they work? 23

What else? 24

Just how about starting your very own hydroponic garden?
....24

Here would be the many benefits of having a hydroponic garden: 25

Plant species which could grow in hydroponics..................26

Hydroponics equipmen 26

5 reasons why you need to offer hydroponics a try.............31

Hydroponic gardening advantages.......................................32

ADVANTAGES OF HYDROPONIC 35

Better space allocation 36

No soil necessary for hydroponics 37

Hydroponics saves water 39

Climate get a grip on 40

Plants grow faster and larger using hydroponics 40

More control over the ph. 41

No more weeds, pests, or infection 42

Hydroponics is less labor-intensive 43

Weather is maybe not really a problem 43

Hydroponics is an excellent hobby 44

Urban farming 45

Could hydroponics be profitable? 45

Is hydroponic food healthful? 46

ADVANTAGES OF HYDROPONICS: PERSONAL PLEASURE 48

Farming for urbanites 48

Benefits of hydroponics 49

A labor-saving device 49

Food for the future 50

Consistency 51

Conservation 52

Earth-friendly gardening 52

THE BENEFITS OF HYDROPONIC GARDENING 53

MOST RECOMMENDED PLANTS FOR A NEW HYDROPONIC GARDEN 63

Tomatoes 63

Lettuce 64

Cucumber..64

Spring blossoms 65

Peppers 65

Spinach 66

Strawberries 66

Blueberries...67

Basil 67

Coriander..68

Growing berries hydroponically 69

Top 9 hydroponic flowers peace lilies 78

TESTING pH 80

Litmus test strips..80

Liquid test 81

Electronic meter..81

Fix ph. 82

When to assess and change the ph. amounts........83

Average ph. ranges for plants 84

Average ph. ranges for nutrient systems............85

Exactly why ph. degrees change from hydroponics systems
....86

The best way to keep the ideal ph. Degrees 87

Benefits of assessing and keeping ph. Degrees......88

**HOW TO DESIGN YOUR OWN HYDROPONIC SYSTEM
AT HOME**...90

Measure 1: Bom - bill of materials 90

Measure 2: produce a house for the pots..................91

Measure 3: aeration..92

Measure 4: sterilization 93

Measure 5: first load 93

Measure 6: pairing plants and prepping moderate 94

Measure 7: beginning from specified 95

Measure 8: care..96

Measure 9: options...97

Measure 10: pests 98

Measure 11: lighting 98

Here are some choices 100

Construction of a deep-water culture system......................105

COMMON MISTAKE TO AVOID IN HYDROPONIC.....109

1. Hydroponics system leaks...............................110

2. Buying inexpensive, insufficient or wrong lighting 111

3. Utilizing the incorrect fertilizer........................113

4. Maybe not keeping things clean 114

5. Not learning as you move.................................115

6. Maybe not tracking the wellness of your plants 115

7. Maybe not tracking and fixing the ph. amount..............116

8. Nutrient deficiency and toxicity 117

9. Employing hard-water from your hydroponics system 119

10. Maybe not tracking ppm / EC / TDS..............120

11. Damaged or allergic pumps and taste nozzles.............122

12. Selecting the wrong growing moderate...........................124

13. Maybe not flushing and refilling the device usually enough 125

14. Assembling an inconvenient hydroponics system........126

15. Plant diseases..127

WHAT IS HYDROPONIC?

If you're looking to try alternative gardening methods that can be made to reveal the premium outcome, hydroponics may be an ideal solution for you personally.

What's hydroponic gardening? The fundamentals of hydroponic gardening

Hydroponic gardening is the thing that occurs whenever a liquid nutrient solution will be devised, and also, the plant has been suspended above and breaks its origins at the clear answer.

Only as plants need sunlight, oxygen, water, carbon dioxide, and minerals, so too do plants grown with hydroponics. Nevertheless, they acquire a number of those needs otherwise than soil-grown plants.

In a dirt increased plant, the plant can survive due to mowing it; its own origins can grow and reach out looking for water and nutrients from the dirt. The dirt itself is there merely to contain the plant at an erect position also to obstruct sunlight out of the roots.

Because it's nourishment and maybe not dirt, which makes it possible for plants to cultivate, making hydroponic gardening potential. When liquid components are flowing around openly at the plant roots, the origins won't have to develop searching for water and food. This lets the majority of the plant's energy to be spent raising the fantastic stuff above the basis. Soil increased plants possess substantially bigger origins, and even less foliage compared to this of a hydroponically grown garden.

Many hydroponic planting occurs at a greenhouse, or any other enclosed structure to permit the many controlled atmospheres. This permits one to better control the lighting, temperatures, insects and weather, etc...

Only about such a thing which may be grown throughout dirt may be increased through this technique. Woody plants such as trees, rose trees, grape blossoms, and trees generally, with the exclusion of banana trees, so do not do too well. Even though seeds from these types of woody-like plants can readily be germinated employing this particular method.

Hydroponic gardening is actually a garden climbing steroids. Whenever you secure the correct mixture of vitamin nutrients to get a certain plant, fresh fruit, or vegetable, then the harvesting period comes even more quickly with a greater return than that of the standard soil approach.

Thus, what's hydroponic gardening? It's gardening without dirt

What's hydroponic gardening?

Hydroponic gardening is your significance of growing plants without using soil. Hydroponic plants have been developed in soapy solutions. All these water solutions comprise the majority of the minerals and additives for plants to grow.

Typically, you can develop hydroponic plants directly from the nutrient solution. Alternately plants may be implanted in an inert growing medium like coconut fibers, rock wool, growing stone, etc...

Hydroponic growing isn't only a favorite hobby pastime; nevertheless, it has become a flourishing small business. When the gardening abilities and methods are mastered precisely, it's possible to literally grow any plant since you need with the hydroponic procedure.

By means of a semi-automatic system, you can simply establish a hydroponic garden or halfway within your home or on the rooftop. When the hydroponic gardening procedure is required on a huge scale, this can grow to be an extremely productive means to make plants for commercial usage.

Unlike developing plants using traditional soil gardening, the main system of blossom plants doesn't need to look for minerals and nutrients from land. All of the naturally-occurring minerals and nutrients are given in the nutrition solution, ready to be furnished into the origin system. For that reason, plants can concentrate on top growth to create more blossoms and fruits as opposed to implementing energy to look for nourishment.

In hydroponic gardening, both carbon and oxygen compounds will also be supplied into the nutrient solution to improve the uptake of nutrients by the main systems. This can help to market faster growth levels and wholesome development of these plants.

Besides that, you'll also possess significantly fewer problems with plant pest and disease problems if growing plants together with hydroponic procedures. Because the majority of the plant pest and disease problems are connected by means of dirt.

Which exactly are hydroponic plants?

Hydroponic plants would be those that are increased in water. This system is becoming more and more popular nowadays because they usually do not require considerable quantities of water gear and also farmlands, which are extraordinarily fertile. Home gardeners and hobby farmers make use of this approach to grow more vegetables during the season. There are a lot of explanations as to why hydroponic plants have gotten so common. We'll look at them one by one.

Grow quicker: hydroponic plants develop older at a faster speed. They return early in the day than conventionally grown plants. Ergo, it lets you save yourself a great deal of time.

Programs less distance: all these crops require quite little room to cultivate as their origins usually do not need to distribute searching for food. That's the reason why they're completely excellent for home gardeners and small scale farmers. There's not any dependence on large areas, and gas prices may also be cut to an enormous scope. This system also makes a simpler and more efficient utilization of greenhouse components.

Automation: among the greatest benefits of hydroponic plants is their growth might be automated with the assistance of timers and remote tracking equipment. Automation results in a decrease over time that's required for the increase of these plants. If you're the master of this a plant, then it supplies you with a great deal of flexibility as you're able to be off in your plant for a very long time period without becoming focused on watering it.

Getting more place under creation: technology may end up being somewhat powerful in arctic lands such as slopes where water can be available is extremely constrained. For that reason, with the assistance of hydroponics technologies, these lands might be turned into productive.

Pests: the hydroponic system uses a sterile growing medium, and that's the reason why hazards due to weeds and pests have been decreased substantially or even completely expunged. If you can find not any pests to bargain with, using pesticides will probably be reduced too. Hence, the machine may end up being cheaper in addition to environmentally favorable.

HYDROPONICS

Hydroponics is famous because it's a number of special benefits for your own gardener. First of all, it saves money by enabling the gardener to recycle any water that's used. And, considering that the nutrients are consumed better, and commanded entirely by the gardener, then the total cost of the compost is significantly reduced. Additionally, plant yields increased in hydroponics are very stable and generally high.

Perhaps the best benefit of hydroponics may be a simple fact it may be grown inside, this means your gardening is not any longer confined by the growing season in that you decide to cultivate it. Therefore, in the midst of winter, then you will grow plants that are strong and healthy.

Why do plants increased using hydroponics grow faster than plants which do not put it to use?

Ostensibly, hydroponics provides the plant what it requires, as it requires. It follows your plants may grow at the fastest rate, which their genetics allows. When then your plant is grown at a standard, soil-based ecosystem, hydroponically grown plants grow at a significantly faster speed and frequently appear fitter.

How hard will it be to use hydroponics equipment?

The potency of electronics is based on the art of the gardener. In the event that it's possible to discover the right ph., increasing moderate, and technology, then you might possibly be astounded at the outcome. That said, electronics gear isn't fundamentally hard to make use of. A fundamental understanding of this gear, together with somewhat of technical understanding, will soon be adequate to meet virtually any gardener. These details can easily be located on the web.

But if you'd like to learn it, then you may need to have a look at a few of the advanced sources of advice, like novels and application kits. For some folks, acquiring the data to cultivate the most useful plants with hydroponics is among the fascinating components of gardening.

HYDROPONIC GARDENING SYSTEM

Whether your interest is located in developing flowers or veggies, the hydroponic gardening system will be right for you. It's simple to start, lower-priced and highly efficient and private, and also very rewarding diversion or overdue that'll reveal the best return, tastes, and colors to what you may grow. Whether you're gardening for pleasure, for the benefit, you get to reap the advantages of hydroponic gardening without even costing too much.

When you have a large backyard, a little one, or even are living at a level with only a handful of window boxes, this may be the beginning of a rather enjoyable pastime for you personally.

A concise history of hydroponics

Hydroponics comes in 2 Greek words, "hydro" meaning water and "panics" meaning labor, the idea which has existed for centuries. Two ancient functioning cases of this method would be the Babylon hanging gardens and the china floating gardens.

Are there really benefits to using hydroponics?

The expansion speed on a hydroponic plant is regarded as between 30-50 percent faster than the usual soil-grown plant. Even the additional oxygen at the hydroponic growing medium will help stimulate root development. The nutrition at a hydroponic system has been mixed with water and also delivered directly into the origin system at which these nutrients have been delivered into the moderate a few times daily. The hydroponic plant takes almost no energy to discover and divide these food nutritional elements. The plant subsequently uses this energy to allow it to grow faster and produce greater blossom or fresh fruit, which subsequently provides a far increased return. Generally, plants grown hydroponically are fitter and more joyful plants, and it is a fantastic thing. I am confident that you would agree.

Hydroponic systems

There are two kinds of hydroponic techniques, which can be active or passive. An energetic approach transfers the nutrient solution through a pump to nourish the vegetable or plant. A passive system counts on the development or gastrointestinal actions of this developing medium used. The nutrient solution will be consumed by the moderate and passed along into the roots.

You want to purchase or make a method your self

Can I buy one or build one? Both have their values. Obtaining a relatively inexpensive system will permit one to secure the toes wet, which may provide you a hands-on method of understanding how operates functions. Whereas, if you're mechanically minded, subsequently construction one will provide you more gratification but will need more time to install. The final effect of the course is the exact same.

Which exactly are hydroponic grow tents?

Growing vegetables and plants have been a favorite pastime for lots of men and women. The debut into hydroponics has changed how that people have begun to consider plant growth because with no demand for dirt opens a wealth of chances. Growing vegetables and plants in grow stalls and grow-boxes are all great methods of earning the use of hydroponics, giving them the nourishment that they desire without dirt or compost. Additional added benefits of using hydroponic grow tents would be that only, less time and less space is required. You additionally more control within the plant's environment like root and humidity zone temperature.

Exactly what exactly are they?

An increase kayak is generally square-shaped, just like a box also can be lined with specially-commissioned complete blackout white / dark / white sheeting for elevated light (lumen) levels in the tent. They have been normally quite simple to establish and therefore are generally quite inexpensive, which range from approximately # 40- # 600. The inside walls of these tents can help purify lighting while the walls onto the surface will probably absorb the warmth. There are several diverse sizes and styles of grow tents readily available; my advice would be always to decide on the best matching size for where you're likely to store it. The simple fact that they are able to fit wherever you want them will be just a fantastic advantage, which usually means they are able to be almost employed by anybody, anywhere.

Just how can they work?

Hydroponic grow tents permit you to regulate every feature of the plant / vegetable environment to let it grow at maximum efficacy. Including controlling heat, light, and water. Having control of these factors implies you could grow just about any plant potential since you're able to mimic precise plant surroundings. Just once a plant gets got the ideal amount of nourishment and sunlight, is it healthy and solid. With hydroponics grow kayak, you may even place tanks up for different kinds of plants to be increased at exactly the exact same moment.

What else?

Hydroponic grow tents are also quite environmentally friendly and may help you save you plenty of cash as weatherproof systems expect a good deal less water compared to traditional gardening. To conserve electricity, you're able to set timers on every one of your fans, heaters, and lights. This cannot merely help with your power bills; it's likewise quite vital for that plant since possibly give your plants a suitable quantity of heat and light.

Just how about starting your very own hydroponic garden?

If you like to garden but confront several issues like limited distance, pests, or improper climate, subsequently hydroponics can be the answer. Hydroponics enables you to raise your garden inside with excessively substantial success prices.

Now, hydroponics is now a pastime for many people, on account of this ease of its own function and also the advantages it's in comparison with the usual means of gardening.

Here would be the many benefits of having a hydroponic garden:

You do not have to have a lot of space to grow your crops. Hydroponics occupies a tiny space and nearly lets you set it anywhere you see fit.

There's no requirement for a great deal of water because there's not any dirt for your water to become consumed until it reaches the plant's origins. Hydroponics is perfect for areas with water restrictions. Using hydroponics conserves water when your warm water a normal garden; just 10 percent of the water that you use will wind up in your plant roots.

You may invest as little time as you can be maintaining your hydroponics garden. Once you've created your garden, you need to devote just a while to the nutrient remedy. No weeds!

You do not have to be burdened with fleas and also locate the right solution or plant diseases such as mosquitoes. Your hydroponics garden could be maintained inside far from these dreadful problems.

Plant species which could grow in hydroponics

There are many quantities of crops which it's possible for you to grow in a backyard. It's possible to create vegetables, herbs like tomatoes, lettuce, cucumbers, peppers; you are able to grow your favorite blossoms or fruit.

Hydroponics may increase the huge majority of plants; however, do remember that plants which rise ought to really be given extra aid.

Hydroponics equipmen

Hydroponic gardening gear can be obtained at the huge most gardening stores. It's not going to hurt to do a small on the web researching the market before seeing the stores; this helps to ensure that you find the most effective services and products for the lowest deals. You might even buy your equipment online.

Lighting at a hydroponics garden is very crucial. The light ensures that the increase in one's garden. It's possible to obtain the different parts from the store of your liking, or you are able to obtain the whole climbing system. The whole growing system comprises all the essential components of your garden, such as lights, fans, timers, etc...

Hydroponic gardening is a thrilling hobby

Everybody has hobbies they like through their pleasurable. Some could have more than 1 hobby. Well, this really is one for all those arborists and anglers, one of the people. Strive indoor hydroponic gardening within a fascinating avocation. In the event that you like gardens and making things grow, then you definitely may cherish indoor gardening.

Hydroponic gardening is precisely exactly like normal gardening, except there isn't any clutter at all. There's not any dirt involved with indoor gardening. Have you seen the renowned Babylon hanging gardens? This really is among the seven wonders of the planet and might be the oldest record we now have of indoor hydroponic gardening at the real history of humanity.

Today, not many individuals possess the means to develop something as extravagant as a this-worldly miracle; however, we are able to grow our personal miniature hanging gardens at a hydroponic greenhouse. That is precisely the exact same task as a greenhouse; however, it's hydroponic because each one the plants have been grown using air, light, and water.

That's correct. No dirt is necessary. This really is what indoor gardening is really all about. Growing your favorite fruits and vegetables at a hydroponic greenhouse has turned into the latest craze among anglers. All you have to accomplish if you're considering moving right down to the community yard and garden shop and check out each the wonderful hydroponic kits. Or it is possible to create your very own. But my advice to get a newcomer is to secure one of those hydroponic kits. A lot of men and women utilize one of 2 basic hydroponic kits: the ebb and flow hydroponic apparel or the profound culture hydroponic kit. All these are simple basic hydroponic kits that have all you will need to begin your own hydroponic greenhouse. You may surely have to obtain additional lights and also more nutritional solutions in the event you opt to enlarge your hydroponic greenhouse. Nevertheless, while in the very long term, it's a fantastic investment.

Research reveals that create grown at a hydroponic greenhouse is, in fact, smarter, juicier, and much more wholesome than the store-bought produce. An additional bonus is that you'll find no pesticide issues commonly encountered by external anglers. There are hardly any pests at the rainwater. This consequently ensures there isn't any requirement for dangerous and harmful insecticides and pesticides. One other fantastic benefit is that using hydroponic kits, so you will grow your favorite veggies and fruits throughout the year. Wow! How amazing is that! I am talking about you could grow your own food, protect your loved ones and yourself from harmful compounds, and revel in your favorite foods at any time through the year.

Indoor gardening really is a fantastic hobby. Not merely is there almost no clutter, no substances, also as far as the eye can easily observe numerous advantages. You have to develop a garden, that can be something which you adore, and lose all of the drawbacks and headaches which normally arrive with gardening. Therefore, in the event that you would like to try out something fresh, go out. Catch a few of your own friends, go to the shop and purchase some hydroponic kits also install your very own hydroponic greenhouse. Then relax and revel in your favorite foods any-time you'd like.

Reasons to grow plants hydroponically

If you are a gardener that you may love the work which goes into fostering plants. Does this draw the ideal soil type however there are sometimes lots of raking, hoeing, tilling as well as other work which goes to keeping up the soil. Then there's the wedding along with also the time and effort that goes into keeping pests away.

Hydroponically grown plants fix these issues since there's not any soil. The plants have been grown in an aggregate that might be anything out of small curved rocks, cracked tiles, perlite, or vermiculite. For that reason, there aren't any additives or cutworms to fret about, no toxic additives without a weeding. You simply need to be worried about keeping the plants watered to routine bases - however; this stress can be looked after with a semi-automatic pump system into your timer. You're able to continue to keep your plants watered at regular intervals as well as carry on a break for a couple of weeks without even fretting about coming home into shriveled up plants that are dead.

Hydroponically grown plants flourish both outside and inside of the home. The nutrient-rich water, coupled with less devastation by fleas, means that you have more reverted returns without waste. They grow well in pure sunlight and artificial lighting. A hydroponic apparatus can be mobile, which makes it simple to create the plants inside throughout the harsh winters. In reality, as a hydroponic unit spreads nutritional elements evenly into each plant, and also the sap escalating aggregate lets air circulate openly, you may ensure everything develops quicker and ripens quicker, producing often times that the return of soil-grown plants across precisely the exact same moment.

In case you have tasted berries out of the supermarket, you might have pointed out they will have rough skins and the absence of taste of homegrown tomatoes. Farmers choose seeds that produce vegetables with skins that are tough that will help machine harvesting, shipping, and sorting. And they're frequently harvested until they tear to guarantee an extended shelf life span. Quality is sacrificed for volume. Homegrown plants, especially those who are hydroponically grown, have superior supplements and also a fuller flavor.

Plants grown at the grocery store tend to be hauled during a very long space diminishing their freshness and contributing to their own cost. With the growth in petroleum prices and enlarging cities gobbling agricultural property, the price of food is very likely to spike as time goes by. Could it be any wonder more and more folks are using hydroponics to cultivate their particular? Hydroponically grown fruits and veg aren't just healthy; more and more bountiful, they are able to help save you a great deal of money in the long run when providing you with the pride of developing something yourself.

5 reasons why you need to offer hydroponics a try

Were you aware that hydroponic gardening is becoming common? Lots of men and women are turning into the particular gardening into their long run so as to have fresh, healthful food in their own tables year-round.

Hydroponic gardening advantages

Inch. You can garden year-round, which means you get new vegetables and herbs all year round. If you're gardening exactly the hydroponic manner, then you definitely won't do with more fresh vegetables throughout winter. And better still, you may not need to pay for the higher price to generate flow from the other continent. All year round gardening - year old round fresh produce in your own desk.

1. No dirt is employed in hydroponics. Usually, plants burn up a great deal of these energies, sending out their roots into the dirt looking for nourishment. Hydroponics feeds the nutritional elements straight into the roots. This usually means that the plant gets greater energy to expend growth and also a higher return of produce. Additionally, the hydroponic plant won't grab infections which come in ordinary soil.

2. You can backyard at a tiny distance indoors. Actually, hydroponic gardening would be your most effective achieved inside. Therefore, irrespective of your deficiency of yard, you may be an inside gardener.

3. Your backyard will be very exact and controlled. With hydroponics, the gardener controls the number of light and nutrients which the plants receive. As you may end up an inside gardener, then you do not need to require the sum of rain and sun falling in your own garden as you can do in the event that you're gardening outdoors.

4. Hydroponic gardens are a breeze to establish. Kits can be bought, or you could buy the equipment you want from the community garden shop. Some supplies may also be purchased in the reduction shop. It is possible to opt to expend somewhat or a lot - based on how complicated you'd like your collection up to become. You may take a hydroponic garden in such a thing from plastic bottles into a gazebo to a tub. You are able to splurge and buy one among those hydroponics packs out there.

Warning: don't jump on the nutritional supplement solution you supply for the plants. Plants grown in dirt derive their follow minerals in this dirt. Ensure that you make use of a fantastic nutrient solution, which includes those trace minerals init. The nutrition that you purchase needs to be made designed for hydroponics.

ADVANTAGES OF HYDROPONIC

Imagine if I told you there was a way to cultivate plants faster, larger, and with just 5 percent of their water normally required.

Many folks would presume that this is hopeless.

And hydroponics lets you perform exactly this.

Hydroponics is a method for developing plants without dirt, using just water, also a nutrient solution, and also moderate to carry the plants in place. Even though various sorts of water civilization have now already been practiced for a few thousand decades, it's just from the past 100 years which the science supporting hydroponics was fully comprehended.

It has allowed both nationally and commercial growers to cultivate plants in fresh techniques that have special pros and cons.

This guide will tell you about the favorable elements of hydroponics, which have definitely resulted in the fast-growing marketplace for hydroponic cultivation.

Hydroponics is a part of a wider drive to increase agricultural efficiency, return, and lower the price of food creation. Domestic hydroponics has grown near this particular, with a rising amount of enthusiasts growing all sorts of plants in the home.

Read on to find some of these most attractive capabilities of hydroponics.

Better space allocation

Plants growing hydroponically need 20 percent less distance than plants grown from dirt. This usually means that you may grow plants in a specified distance, or you may grow plants in tiny spaces at which it wouldn't be practical to cultivate soil established plants.

It has striking consequences for your farming business, where most plants have been grown in high priced indoor greenhouses, where efficient usage of distance is vital to realize a fantastic return on investment.

The main reason is that hydroponic plants require less distance compared to soil-grown plants as well as the origins would not need to distribute over the ground to look for water and nutrients. Water and nutrients are sent into the origins directly, either intermittently or depending upon the average person hydroponic technique. Roots are somewhat more streamlined because of this and may grow closer together. As less distance becomes necessary, farmers can create considerably higher yields, without infrastructure.

No soil necessary for hydroponics

The thought of developing create without dirt was a foreign idea; however, it has become a real possibility for both commercial and domestic growth.

Growing plants without dirt have numerous benefits.

There's a wide variation in soil quality in 1 location to another location, and lots of plants have strong preferences for a specific land type. If you don't need this dirt type available, then it can be costly and labor-intensive to export suitable soil or change your current soil.

There are a few places across the planet that have usage of dirt or where the soil is constrained. One of those earliest commercial farming operations was about wake island in the pacific. This really is a rugged atoll, which doesn't need any dirt acceptable for growing plants.

This island has been used as a refueling stop for Pan American airlines from the 1930s. It'd have been prohibitively costly to import fresh produce; therefore, hydroponics was used to cultivate the equipment demanded.

Other nations with restricted land, such as rocky or desert regions, wouldn't longer be confined with just how much they can rise. This is actually a motivational factor for its transition into hydroponics, that is why it's being contemplated the cultivation for their future. The chances for farming are significantly improved in such locations. They can cut the requirement to import fresh produce and may decrease water consumption, which may be a concern in most nations.

Hydroponics saves water

Hydroponic plants may develop with only 510 percent of the water needed after growing together with the dirt. This is definitely an immense advantage in water resources and also a leading ecological gain of hydroponic cultivation.

Hydroponics capitalizes on re-circulated water, in which plants consume what they desire, and runoffs are recorded and returned to this device. The water lost is out of flows and evaporation, but an efficient installation may minimize these when at all possible.

Some hydroponic methods are utilizing a lot more technology to decrease water waste much farther. The fact is that the entire water which plants carry by using their origins, 95 percent with the is invisible to the atmosphere.

Because of this, some industrial hydroponics systems are utilizing water vapor condensers to fully capture this water and then return into the machine.

International food manufacturing proceeds to grow year on year, also so is consuming more oxygen than ever. Until we use technologies such as hydroponics to empower more sustainable agriculture, then we're endangering the environment of the world.

Climate get a grip on

Hydroponic surroundings deliver complete control within the climate. It's possible to adjust the temperature, light intensity, and duration, and also the makeup of the atmosphere, all in harmony in what's vital for optimum expansion. This produces a path to cultivate produce no matter season, meaning farmers may optimize production throughout the year, and consumers will get services and products each time they really want.

Plants grow faster and larger using hydroponics

What's astonishing about hydroponics is that the capacity for expansion. You presume that jelqing would contribute to lower returns; however, the alternative is correct. There's scope to rise faster than dirt, eased by the means to regulate humidity, humidity, light, and nourishment.

Creating perfect requirements for plants receive the best number of nutritional elements which can be found from direct contact with the origins. Plants thus will not need to waste valuable energy, searching for diluted nutrients from the dirt. As an alternative, they could alter their attention toward producing and growing veggies, leading to better growth rates and larger plants.

More control over the ph.

Ph. amounts are sometimes overlooked by growers; however, it's a crucially important component of farming, which makes certain your plants may access the right levels of nourishment that they need for balanced growth.

Unlike developing plants in the land, crucial minerals for expansion are totally found in the expanding solution. The ph. of the solution might be corrected readily and quantified accurately to make certain the optimal ph. is kept whatsoever times.

Ensuring optimum ph. will improve the plant's capability to uptake minerals that are essential. In the case of ph., ranges vary a lot; plants reduce the capacity to consume nutrients. Even though some plants flourish in slightly acidic growth surroundings, ph. levels should range between 5.5 -7. Growers could be a good idea to analyze optimal ph. degrees for your plant under consideration, also consider just how hydroponic growth permits effective management.

No more weeds, pests, or infection

Weeds are frustrating to eliminate from the soil and certainly will affect the development of the plants you're cultivating. With hydroponics, they're no more an issue. In the same way, soil-borne pests aren't just an issue.

Because of the dirt environment, most hydroponic growth systems usually do not require pesticides, which may produce the product more beneficial for individual consumption preventing the conditions that pesticides could cause the setting. At a closed system of hydroponic cultivation, it is simple to assume charge of the nearby factors.

Hydroponics is less labor-intensive

Although the installation costs of a hydroponic process are definitely higher priced, either for domestic or business usage, the labor involved with fostering plants is significantly decreased. It frees up time for you to concentrate on additional tasks, as opposed to tilling, hoeing, plowing, etc. In addition, it can reduce running costs with time, but this is dependent upon the device involved.

Weather is maybe not really a problem

Whether employing a straightforward hydroponic method to grow a couple of tomatoes in your window sill or owning a business hydroponic head-light, you're able to eliminate a key source of doubt in plants that are growing. Because most hydroponic plants have been increased either inside or in greenhouses, and all of the nutrients and water required are supplied by hand, you get rid of the doubt that includes unpredictable weather.

Even the sun might be a concern, even as artificial grow light may replace or supplement the sun. Employing artificial grow lights will allow one to cultivate plants throughout the year. As for me, I utilize led grow lights that will allow me to grow tomatoes and salad greens throughout the year. When hard to overcome fresh salad when you require it.

Hydroponics is an excellent hobby

I developed a fascination with hydroponics as a hobby a range of years back, and I definitely love it. You're able to begin growing plants using hydroponics for hardly any upfront price. There are tons of both DIY and pre-built systems you are able to utilize, which is quite scalable.

You can begin by growing only two or one plants in your own window sill. This was the way I started and allowed me to learn a lot about what plants will need to grow and flourish. You're able to scale up things out there, and there's really no limitation to just how much you are able to take this avocation.

Even though I love outside gardening also, I love having greenery inside my home, and it's rewarding to develop veggies and salad greens throughout every season I may use to nourish my family members.

Urban farming

Hydroponics is increasing, also in 2015, its own international value was projected at roughly $21.4 billion. You'll find huge worldwide modifications on the horizon, and which can be put to quicken the development of the farming procedure.

These modifications will probably be released out of requirement, to adapt a rapidly expanding world populace. We use a huge percentage of available property for growing plants; therefore, new farming methods need to be built to increase to create other properties acceptable for growing plants. Vertical urban agriculture is a potential farming system that simplifies the dilemma of insufficient distance and works extremely nicely with hydroponics.

Could hydroponics be profitable?

Although hydroponics is getting significant press attention, the majority are left wondering if it's a commercially workable clinic. I presume that the brief answer is yes, according to the large industrial operations in functioning now.

Hydroponic farming is deemed costly as a result of elevated costs; however, there are lots of methods to keep down costs.

Stacked rack systems certainly are a terrific illustration of cost-cutting efforts, but these may impair heat, humidity, and heat. It's a sensible choice to research if the cost is a restrictive factor; nevertheless, you could wind up getting sourcing testing and parts configurations. Growers are more sensible to exploit led light technology, together with enough par value to keep up nutritious production. Even though high par lights cost more initially, regain your investment by growing high-yielding plants, stated in shorter spans.

Is hydroponic food healthful?

Fundamentally, it all depends on the nutritional supplement solution. When veggies get the nutrition that they need to cultivate effortlessly, hydroponics could produce food equally as healthful as if grown in dirt.

Marion Nestle, professor of nutrition new york university, considers hydroponics has come quite a way, promising that the nutrient content of leafy greens grown hydroponically falls well within normal limits and so are sometimes even greater!

The nutrient material of these plants may vary based upon the nutrition used; however, all recordings are much from what the plants increased in this manner are as nutritious and healthy as the ones grown in the ground.

What's helpful about hydroponic development is your capability to raise plant nutritional levels by simply the addition of what's required into this clear answer. It's possible to essentially add anything is needed, whether calcium, calcium, iron, magnesium, or calcium, such as. The capacity to modulate nutrient concentration in this manner creates a range to grow plants that are more exceptional.

Very important to recall, you will find many external factors to think about, irrespective of the growing procedure, like the period of the year, harvested, just how long after harvesting plants become eaten, and also how plants are managed. Nutrient articles vary based on those variables; however, the main point is that weight reduction growth may produce just as healthy, if not healthy, foods than traditional procedures.

ADVANTAGES OF HYDROPONICS: PERSONAL PLEASURE

Farming for urbanites

Can you reside in a condominium or high tech flat? No sheet of ground to call your very own? Perhaps not a terrace? Then hydroponics will be your answer for you personally! Brand new, yummy vegetables or medicinal or culinary compounds in your own spare bedroom. And sometimes possibly a cupboard.

In case you are restricted to a wheelchair, then hydroponics may be the ideal way to delight in a garden. The planting beds are all traditionally located, just the ideal height for simple access. What a great and satisfying hobby (and sometimes maybe vocation) this is to you!

Benefits of hydroponics.

Hydroponics is a soothing, gratifying, stress-dissolving hobby. It is an escape. Put a seat right next to an own unit. Often your own babies, train them up and speak with them. Play jazz, classical, or modern music, in their opinion. And sometimes maybe a hard stone if you'd like to buy it. Who cares what people think?

Hydroponic gardening sets you in contact with character in a beautiful way. And remember that the "wow" variable... Your own family and friends will hold you in amazement for the agricultural accomplishments.

A labor-saving device

· listed here is the very best portion of no weeds!!! When you've ever needed a dirt garden, then you will comprehend how powerful that really is. No weeds, no weed-killers, no backbreaking labor, no grief when you return from a vacation to discover an overgrown weed patch wherever your melons were.

· there is no tilling, plowing, hoes, wheelbarrows, or bags of mulch to take care of. Ugh!

Food for the future

Superior taste & nutrition

· when dwelling hydroponics first surfaced on the scene several decades past, frankly, the produce wasn't that yummy. But that is all changed as a result of modern strategies and superior nutritional elements. Grocery-bought veggies are bred to boat rough, continue for weeks, also look amazing on the plate. Nevertheless, they're dull! Blah! Tasteless! Hydroponic vegetables are more tender and delicate. Plus, they taste great!

· this has been demonstrated that hydroponically grown veggies might have around 50 percent more vitamin (especially vitamin a, all b-complexes, e, and c) than normal plants *.

As green as it gets

Consistency

· together with soil-based gardening, you're subject to land quality, both the weather and wind, bugs, and soil-borne diseases. With hydroponics, you might have considerably more control over the garden. With more consistent outcomes.

· hydroponics also lends itself beautifully to automation (auto-pilot). Set it and forget it! Well, perhaps not exactly.

Conservation

· you're going to find a lot higher return in the hydroponics garden, and also the developing cycle is much briefer. After getting the hang of this and also learn how to maximize, it is possible to get three times just as much produce in the indoor climbing storyline.

· we hear often about the lack of water and also the requirement to store it. Well, hydroponics simply uses 1/20 into 1/30 that the sum of water just as conventional, soil-based gardening. It's poisonous, and every molecule of water has been poured into the maximal. You use less fertilizer, too. More cash into your pocket.

Earth-friendly gardening

Soil-born pests, fungi viruses, and infections are eradicated entirely within a hydroponic system. You usually garden indoors or inside a climate-controlled greenhouse, and that means you won't have a plague of locusts descend for you personally, or candy small bunnies munching in your own precious butter crunch lettuce.

In case you have an invasion of whitefly or red spider mites, then you may take charge of one's streamlined garden and expel these pests readily and always without dyes. Given that is truly organic!

THE BENEFITS OF HYDROPONIC GARDENING

Hydroponic systems supply nutrients directly into the plants by means of a nutrient-rich blend of oxygen and water. This is an even far more aftereffect of far compared to dirt since most of the nutritional elements have been directly delivered into the roots as opposed to being squeezed through dirt, which could leach some nourishment until they reach the plant. This effect provides you fitter and more plants compared to plants grown in the ground.

The benefits of home gardeners are numerous. As a result of limited space, you can scale off your garden while getting amazing results. Additionally, this enables individuals who usually do not need access to dirt in any way, flat dwellers, to move right ahead and also have a garden at the space they are able to afford to use. Additionally, many folks can have lousy weather or even bad dirt where they live, and also this method totally works round it.

As an additional benefit, hydroponic gardening is cleaner, better, and more durable than conventional gardening; also, it might be year-round. Your hydroponic system may virtually eliminate the threat of germs and eradicate the dependence on pesticides, that may be damaging to your health and fitness.

As a pastime, hydroponic gardening is definitely satisfying. You're almost guaranteed to have an excellent effect because you eat your own edibles or cut on your flowers from your own body that you've grown yourself. An additional plus is a fact that it could be applied as a solution to contact your child and give them an excellent connection with making their own food and also undergoing the bounty they help produce.

The expense of constructing your hydroponic gardening process is fairly cheap. Many bits necessary for an excellent hydroponic system are seen in the community hardware shop, and some of those parts, if any, are specialization, hard to detect, or even exceptionally pricey. If you'd like, it is also possible to get the most of one's apparel on the web, maybe not needing to leave your home order your plants.

The general size and layout of your hydroponic system are going to undoubtedly be driven by your own growth plans and open distance.

Hydroponics is utilized to increase nearly any such thing. You're able to grow berries, roses, orchids, angel's breath, plus even more. When it is really a plant, then it could be in a position to cultivate in a pristine environment.

The key to hydroponic gardening would be that the dirt isn't required in the event that you provide the proper nourishment into the plants. Soil is unnecessary, provided that you send the ideal mixture of nourishment. The last advantage is that hydroponic systems provide nourishment more effortlessly compared to dirt.

A greenhouse gives you many benefits of hydroponic gardening

Hydroponic gardening is the science of growing plants in a controlled environment with dirt - clear of soil-borne diseases and pests. Hydroponically grown plants have been increased in greenhouses under closely controlled and monitored states. Gravel is often applied as a medium to encourage the plant's origins over the greenhouse. Watchfully mixed nutritional elements are subsequently occasionally fed into plants in liquid form - an approach identified as a sub-irrigation culture. Once seedlings are planted, virtually most of this work is achieved by automation. These hydroponic greenhouses detectors within the dirt are utilized to figure out once the plants want more nutrition and twist on the pumps, so giving the plants that the only right quantity of solution.

All these hydroponically grown crops would be the exact nutrients necessary for rapid growth and volume generation. Some hydroponic gardeners utilize special tanks that can be created from big drums, which can be cut by 50 percent. Underneath every half is brazed using the metal tube. And the hose is clamped to a single end of this tube. The opposite end is mounted on an identical tube that's inserted to a little can.

In the tanks could be painted. Asphalt established paint so as to reduce metal surfaces from corrosion. The tanks are full of little sized sand pellets.

The hydroponic gardening procedure starts together with 'placing the tanks' by starting seedlings in carefully prepared paper cups filled with vermiculate to permit the hydroponic way to input. Once the plants have been launched, the entire cup needs to be set inside the gravel. The plant's origins have been irrigated from underneath as fluid flows down the nozzle and then into the dirt. The technique is installed to be certain the plants are moist but not bombarded using an alternative in higher than a couple of seconds.

The advantages of hydroponic gardening in a greenhouse are many different. When plants are grown hydroponically, harvest yields are raised radically over agriculture. By way of instance, an acre of a property may yield to the heaps of berries. The very same quantity of distance will return 60 to 300 heaps when grown hydroponically. A carrot harvest grown in a hydroponic greenhouse can yield a rise of 12,000 pounds within lettuce.

Hydroponic gardening offers additional benefits besides increased harvest yield. The hydroponic greenhouse environment expands the growing season and doesn't want heavy labor. And of course the obvious - there is certainly not any demand for rainwater dirt!

Appropriate dieting is quite important to maintain a wholesome living. In a hectic and busy schedule, you consistently take some time to consume your lunch or catch a very simple bite. Now, getting food will be much faster, though it could be costly sometimes, it is worth every cent. Most of us would like to eat nutritious food, which gives us the ability to escape the daily undertaking. However, would you ever wonder exactly what food is about it? What's it made, and what exactly was it made from?

Your treasured green veggies may be planted anywhere. You will worry if it's safe to eat it. Plants grow if they're not well cared for. Nevertheless, the probability of eating those veggies which develop anywhere is quite high. Roots of plants consume nutrients from the ground, which leads to its own growth. Once the minerals and nutrients have been consumed by the roots, then it's spread to the leaves to the maturation of the plant. But the minerals and nutrients originating from the ground cold are polluted, which would lead to vomiting to the plants to people who'll eat it.

The scientist created a method of developing plants that don't demand dirt. It's referred to as a hydroponic program. Hydroponics can be a normal technique in mathematics research and instruction. This procedure encourages the rise of vegetables as well as other plants with outside lands. Since the significant component in plants is

58

minerals and nutrients, this particular machine has a method of providing those demands for your plants in a controlled and milder manner. Even the hydroponic system can be costly for farmers that are regular; however, it also produces quite a good benefit. Through this procedure, folks are ensured that the veggies that they eat are harmless and also more healthful. Ergo farmers utilizing this method can benefit their consumer confidence and cause higher revenue.

As recognition of the benefits of this hydroponic system develops into our farmers' mind. The growing fruits and vegetables that you take in will probably be a lot longer progress. You don't need to fret about those germs which the plants can acquire since they're implanted and well cared for at a controlled atmosphere. You'll be assured that even should you not prepare the meals that you eat, it's still healthy, nutritious, and clean. Organic meals will become safer and enjoyable to consume

Pinpointing the benefits of hydroponic gardening

Such gardening doesn't require one to worry about crucial elements like having not enough or a lot of drinking water. You don't need to worry about dirt issues or if to fertilize and the total amount of nutrition to employ. Bid farewell to farm and simmer for feel together side dirt consistency. At exactly the exact same time, that you do not need to consider the risk that plants will soon compete for nutrients and water.

Hydroponics can create quite healthful yields. Additionally, this course of action is clean, dependable, and effortless. Nourishment is infused directly into the origin systems. Because of this, plants grow fast and require just a fifth of their entire distance as the dirt garden process. Hydroponic plants aren't infected by fleas and diseases. Hence, you save your self-concerning soil planning, weeds, and fungicide compounds.

Hydroponics necessitate 90% less water in addition to fertilizers when compared with conventional plants that are growing. The water utilized within this system visits the plants with no potential for over-watering. On the other hand, water from agriculture gets the propensity to elope and clogs away the fertilizers. It's practically 100 percent absolutely free of contamination. There's not any agricultural escape. In traditional farming, the excess fertilizers comprise elevated rates of phosphorus, potassium, and phosphorous. Whether this excess would go into the water or rivers tributaries, the algae will probably eventually become uncontrollable. This will slough away the oxygen out of water sources and also kill any kind of life.

The increase rate is faster. It might generate as much as 5 times that the product for every single square foot. The plants profit out of water, oxygen, and nourishment. Hydroponics can be a tantamount to cheap distribution mechanism for nourishment with lower risks with respect to crop.

While crops increase in plain water, there's a requirement to get a smaller level of h2o when compared with this standard procedure. You are able to save yourself financial funds since the sterile elements might be recycled. The nutritional elements have been infused into the water and spread to the roots to get optimal outcomes. Plants stay fresh as such can receive nutritional elements before the final escalating point.

The preliminary investment price for hydroponics is lower compared to conventional farming processes. It could function as an ideal alternative for traditional farming, especially in very arid regions, mountainous regions, and remote locations. It is easy to grow plants much in ice-covered property since there isn't any requirement to make use of garden dirt.

MOST RECOMMENDED PLANTS FOR A NEW HYDROPONIC GARDEN

Hydroponics is a method of growing plants, even in water, minus soil. Minerals and nutrients have been added into the water at optimal levels; therefore, the plants may devote their energy to producing vegetables and fruits and end in a bigger return.

Using hydroponics, you may grow nearly anything. Here are our top ten veggies & fruits to cultivate at a hydroponic greenhouse:

Tomatoes

Vining crops such as berries are perfect for indoor gardens that they demand a little bit of ground space, and you will have room to prepare them upward into the ceiling. Having the ability to see and manage the nutrition that the plant received empowers the grower to relish a continuous harvest all through the year without sacrificing taste. Banners are a rich supply of vitamins c and folic acid. They feature strong antioxidants that help protect against the potential for cardiovascular disease, cancer, and diabetes.

Lettuce

Lettuce is a leading choice for hydroponic anglers since it needs little distance, little care, and also you're able to harvest leaves since it develops. You're going to receive your very first crop in only a matter of weeks once you are able to enjoy the advantages of your very first crispy harvest. Lettuce is really minimal calorie veg which contains phytonutrients that possess health-promoting and disease-preventing properties. Full of vitamins c and k also comprise minerals like calcium, iron potassium, and magnesium that are critical for the human body metabolic rate.

Cucumber

Water adoring fruits create a fantastic choice for the hydroponic garden. Given enough distance and encourage cucumbers will expand abundantly. Cucumbers are high in micro-elements iron, magnesium, magnesium, potassium, magnesium, and zinc. Additionally, they contain vitamins b, b, c, and folic acid. These elements make smoothies successful at cleaning your system from cholesterol, reducing the process of aging, and regulating metabolic rate.

Spring blossoms

Spring blossoms are, in reality, very youthful onions chosen earlier; the bulb has to grow and swell. 1 bud can sprout a large number of blossoms and be chosen every three or four weeks! The antioxidants in spring peppers assist in preventing damage to DNA and cell cells by inhibiting the activity of free radicals. Spring onions are filled with vitamins k and c, which are both crucial for healthy bones. Spring blossoms' natural properties are most often utilized to deal with viral diseases like influenza and colds. Additionally, they include vitamins b and a.

Peppers

Peppers will develop in very similar states to berries, nevertheless increasing evening temperatures and diminishing daylight temperatures improves fresh fruit production once plants reach their adult height. Peppers maybe not just add spice and flavor into your own food but are also low in calories and packed with vitamins and nutrition. Saturated in vitamins c and an and also a terrific source of fiber, folic acid, and potassium provide them great wellness and disease-fighting properties.

Spinach

Exactly like lettuce besides leafy veggies such as lettuce develop nicely in hydroponic techniques. Spinach is fast-growing and successful in the event that you maintain it all harvested. Spinach is a remarkably healthy green leafy vegetable well-known because of its antioxidant properties. It provides iron, protein, minerals, and vitamins. Spinach is a great source of vitamins a, k, c, e, and magnesium, folic acid, aluminum, zinc, and more, which makes one of those healthier green-leafed vegetables moving. It protects the heart and reduces cholesterol and helps with digestion, and reduces aging and gives a rich resource of iron.

Strawberries

Strawberries flourish in moist conditions and expand nicely in hydroponic conditions. Supplying larger fruits than inland and may offer harvest throughout the year. Strawberries are packed with antioxidants and vitamin c that are well-known resistance boosters. They also assist in reducing cholesterol and higher blood pressure.

Blueberries

Blueberries need high polluted soil conditions and so grow in hydroponic problems. Assessing the ph. nutrients and content is a lot easier and is likely to result in a far bigger, much healthier harvest. Blueberries are well-known because of its full of antioxidants that protect the brain and nervous system. They truly are rated among the greatest fruits for providing vitamins and antioxidants necessary for a sound human body.

Basil

Herbs are a really popular option as they need care and may produce a remarkable harvest. Not merely do herbaceous plants offer taste and odor; however, they will have a vast array of health applications. Research shows ginger helps decrease swelling and inflammation; it's full of antioxidants also helps protect against free radicals, which cause aging.

Coriander

Coriander is a superb herb to increase, which just occurs approximately 30 days and can create 2 3 harvests. It needs no unique requirements, even though plenty of lighting will probably provide one of the deepest harvests. Coriander has multiple health benefits. It comprises vitamin c, vitamin, and protein and is still actually a source of potassium, fiber, and iron. It really is known to assist with skin discomfort, higher cholesterol, mouth nausea, digestion, and several different ailments.

25 of the most useful plants for indoor hydroponic gardens growing herbs hydroponically

Imagine having the capability to select fresh herbs once you really want them. This can change, perhaps not only the taste of one's meal but also the nutrient material from the meals you prepare. Additionally, it is important to be aware that even though you'll be able to plant out of seeds in the majority of scenarios, carrying a cutting is nearly always the preferred option. This technique not only receives the plant growing faster but quicker as well.

Growing berries hydroponically

In addition to the aforementioned herbs, you can find several more forms of plants you can grow at a water-based escalating moderate, including a variety of veggies. The majority would be the exact types you'd grow on your outdoor garden, yet many others are an assortment specially designed to cultivate at a more compact space. Bear in mind that if you're consuming your plant and giving it lighter, it is going to grow.

To get the aid of plants such as tomatoes, I like to make use of clay stalks, since they allow the origins to possess a strong grip on something. The table shows only a number of vegetable plants; it is possible to grow hydroponically.

Veggies well worthy of hydroponics taste of hydroponic berries

It is likely that whenever you tell people you are growing hydroponically, then they are going to explain to your things such as:

· there's no flavor

· there are no vitamins

· it is not organic

· it is unhealthy

All these are only several of the reason why people assert they don't really enjoy veggies, which can be grown in plain water. When there's a gap in taste will probably soon be to the standard of the food from the water. Even though berries (for instance) have increased in various areas of dirt, there's a taste gap. The same goes for its content.

There will be individuals who're reluctant to just accept that the simple fact that lots of plants could be increased in this manner, as a few folks are shut minded. Do not waste your own time hoping to influence them; just enjoy your new crops that are grown.

Below is an inventory of plants that can be ideal for growing without any dirt. These can grow quite happily in a hydroponic system.

Now you may understand a lot of these and become growing already. Therefore, why don't you make use of cutting and start growing it into your brand new system? Not just are house plants amazing to possess at a house; however, in addition, they help clean the air by absorbing carbon dioxide. Which of them are you going to decide to try fostering in plain water?

The advantages of growing rings hydroponically in home

When you visit the food store, can you really truly feel as though you're forced to buy the things that they have? Obviously, you might search for some farmers' markets and check around at a few of the specialty shops. But let us be realistic, who's got the opportunity to complete that? Especially for those who have a family and employment, there simply are not enough hours in your afternoon to be conscientious as we all believe we must be.

We all desire to present healthy, fantastic quality food for our loved ones. Every single day there is apparently always a fresh, informative article either on the web or on the news headlines of GMO foods or toxins from the water out of farms. By growing yourself, you recognize what you are eating, and you also realize what's been used to nourish that plant you are bringing into your own desk.

In case you are a gardener, you might balk at the idea of growing plants into exactly what some say is an artificial atmosphere. I sensed exactly the same before I did a little research.

Additionally, it ends up hydroponically grown veggies have the same number of vitamins as the ones grown at the floor. Naturally, that depends upon the caliber of the nutrition you're investing inside their growing household. Nevertheless, the exact same is said for lands. In the event that you grow a plant from the soil that is poor, it'll be with a lack of flavor--whether it develops at all. The nutrition you get from it's going to even be diminished. (organically grown veggies may also vary in vitamin material too.)

Here is a fast listing of a number of the advantages of plants hydroponically:

· you realize where the food came out.

· you are able to prevent any pesticides.

· hydroponic plants generally grow faster compared to those grown in dirt.

· the returns in many cases are more than those grown from the dirt.

· that you never require a garden distance --or even distance in all--to build plants.

· hydroponic plants generally bring fewer bugs and diseases.

· there are not any weeds to pull on.

· hydroponic gardening conserves water.

Tips for growing plants inside hydroponically

Here are a couple of additional strategies and considerations to bear in mind for your own hydroponic garden:

· lighting: only because a plant has been increased in plain water does not necessarily indicate that it will not still require the sun. Especially regarding vegetables and fruits such as tomatoes & many anything with blossoms, you are going to have to either put your plants close to a caked window or determine another means to receive them shinier mild --ideally at least half hours every day. Regrettably, this is sometimes extremely complicated as a result of various spectrums of intensity, light, and power, and of course, different demands of plants.

ph. amount: based on what you are attempting to cultivate, maybe not with the best ph. level of your own water may greatly reduce your plants' capacity to absorb vitamins, carbs, and other nutritional supplements. (as an example, the majority of the herbs mentioned previously flourish in a ph. level which is lower compared to that on tap water) therefore it is critical to look at the perfect ph. preferences of one's plants and fix the water so.

climate/temperature: since most plants prefer a temperature between 60--80°f, it is vital to watch on what cold or hot it receives round your hydroponic garden. Sometimes you will have to guard it against heat generated from the grow lamps or perhaps a nearby radiator. Other times you ought to safeguard them from falling temperatures in winter, though they are inside.

What's a Nutrient Film Technique (NFT)?

Nutrient film technique (nft) can be a lively Xmas system wherein water containing dissolved nutrients is pumped right into an increased menu; therefore, those nutrients may be absorbed by plants while the water moves through their origins. This water is then emptied into a lower reservoir has been finally pumped straight back throughout the expansion tray.

Additionally, it is among the very versatile and popular methods for jelqing and will be especially helpful for fast-paced, lightweight plants such as lettuce--though it isn't quite as effective for growing thicker crops such as berries.

What is the difference between hydroponics, aquaculture, and aquaponics?

It is quick to become confused with the terminology because there is jargon special to various farming methods. Additionally, there are many men and women using the words, which further increases this confusion. In reality, the word aquaculture incorporates plants, which means you are able to observe people can easily be duped by the length of language.

Let us clear-up what we're speaking going to lose some light onto the topic:

· hydroponics: this pertains to growing plants in water that's nutrients and minerals included. For larger plants, frequently clay stalks, coir, perlite, or gravel are traditionally used to encourage the roots. There's not any soil.

· aquaculture: that really is actually the increase of fish, crustaceans, mollusks, aquatic plants, and algae. Fish cultivation, which we've done on our farm, also comes under this category.

· aquaponics: this unites the 2 aspects of aquaculture and hydroponics, with abundant wastewater out of fish or alternative aquaculture activity to enhance the water for those plants. Frequently plants will be expanded along with a tank, tank, or pond, together with fish swimming (and defecating) below.

Why don't you offer hydroponics a strive?

I may think of no reason to not take to with a hydroponic system, even though you employ it in combination with your typical gardening. This usually means that you are able to consume fresh food if you want this, and the food miles work out to approximately 6 feet based on how big your own kitchen. It beats using it flown from the country thousands of kilometers off.

Kiddies will love viewing with the plants growing facing those. They could even be receptive to eating their own greens should they've helped them.

If you're on the lookout for more info about the best way best to establish your own hydroponics system

9 rings to cultivate hydroponics exactly why hydroponic flowers?

Flower gardeners spend hundreds of hours tilling and adapting to the ground. Why this makes blossom gardening appear work, of course, when it takes that much energy, why do you think about growing plants in a hydroponic system?

There are actually many advantages and advantages blossom gardening in hydroponics has overland growing.

Results come considerably quicker; you are able to tailor your nutrition to each plant species; also, you also don't have any weeds, insects, and less disorder to cope with. This produces an up to and including fifty percent faster growth in blossoms, and returns are much more compared to soil development.

With this in mind, now you can grow blossoms all year round, and also then could be costly to get when out of date. You might also provide as numerous cut flower displays around your property as you desire.

Before a comprehensive look at every blossom, below are eight of these top blossoms you may grow on your own system.

· peace lilies

· hoya

· snapdragons

- dahlias

- rex begonias

- carnations

- orchids

- petunia

- zinnia

Top 9 hydroponic flowers peace lilies

Being an indoor plant, the peace lily could be just one of the simplest to take care of. You want the best growing requirements, though. These tropical blossoms are sections of their spathiphyllum family members and are familiar by their dark green leaves and white blossoms.

While we could develop these at a hydroponic system, they don't really like to be more over-watered. They could, in reality, be tolerant of under-watering compared to being too much-drinking water. Peace lilies that grow into a hydroponic system, in many cases, are accommodated versions where they ship small sections to absorb water.

Many manufacturers frequently wait until leaves reveal indications of recurrence prior to flushing; this may prevent more watering. Should they truly be overwatered, it might result in root rot, and also, the plant will probably suffocate.

TESTING pH

As ph. drifts past the ideal degree for plants, numerous problems might appear as clarified. This is why you will need to come up with a program to confirm the ph. of this answer onto a frequent foundation.

You will find an assortment of tools to ascertain ph. degrees, which range from low-cost easy-to-use paper strips along with liquid evaluation kits to high priced high-tech meters available on the industry.

Litmus test strips
Evaluation strips are not any doubt that the lowest priced means of ph. checking on the list of people recorded here. Essentially, you'd dip the strips into the nutrient solution. And the delicate dye of these strips can change color. Assessing along with the ph. color chart will inform you just how basic or acidic the solution is. The drawback of those strips would be it doesn't offer a precise dimension as it's situated on color, assessing onto the strips that will be quite difficult to learn.

If you're news, brief of cash or you also need a simple way, test strips are all good to go.

Liquid test

Like evaluation strips, the fluid test kits have been really simple and easy to utilize. Nonetheless, it offers an extremely accurate and trustworthy outcome of ph. assessing. To make use of it, you'd add a number of those ph. sensitive dye drops into a little cup along with your solution indoors. Check out the color change of the solution with the ph. chart color graph.

The liquid evaluation kits are somewhat costlier compared to evaluation strips; nevertheless, the outcomes are way more accurate. This causes it to be probably the very used ph. assessing system by hobby hydroponic gardeners.

Electronic meter

Whilst the very high-tech procedure of ph. assessing the electronic meter indicates the end result very fast and accurately. The ph. number is going to be published onto your device's screen. Therefore, you should not compare to the color graph. There are certainly a number of digital ph. meters using various sizes and prices. However, the ph. pencil could be popular among hydroponic amateurs. In spite of the very best and fastest ph. dimension of most ph. testing procedures, the electronic meter has the disadvantage to be very costly, and it requires taking excellent care of it. The meter may float following time and reveal lasting outcomes. The ph. pencil needs continuous cleaning and attentive storage to get its own life extension.

It is a fantastic idea to also invest a couple of dollars to get a liquid ph. test strip or kit to double-check the truth of the tube or if the meter breaks.

Fix ph.

You can adjust the ph. level of your solution by simply the addition of a few malic acids to lessen acid, or potassium hydroxide to enhance your own ph.

Many folks bring the ph. down by utilizing white vinegar (acetic acid), uric acid). However, these acids are absolutely feeble, which doesn't attract good long-term ph. reducing effect.

Additionally, there are specially made ph. upward and ph. down solutions that are available in the marketplace. I urge these obtainable solutions since they have been very simple to utilize and bring effects fast. Additionally, it will come with ph. buffers which help re-circulate the ph. into the right levels.

And because you're utilizing acids to correct your own ph. level, you can find a number of words of repeats. Make sure you shield your skin and eyes whenever using antioxidants. Better safe than sorry. Of course, in the event that you might be supposed to combine a concentrated acid into water, never pour water to the acidity.

The acidity will heat and will spit high-temperature acid for your requirements. As an alternative, discard the acid directly into the water, stirring and discovering whether the clear answer becomes hot.

When to assess and change the ph. amounts

The ph. assessing and adjusting measure ought to only be achieved once you've mixed the nutritional elements together with water as soon as you've diffused them and let it circulate all through one's body. That is only because the nutrition compounds will transform the ph. level of their water.

Different hydroponic systems, developing media properly used, nutrients, plant types, and the climate may interrupt the ph. of your strategy long or fast term.

For hydroponic novices, I urge that you assess it daily to understand whether your machine ph. has shifted smoothly or perhaps not. Then correct it appropriately. Experienced hydroponic anglers may understand just how long to test and fix this amount.

The best way to keep up the ph. quantities of hydroponic systems

Average ph. ranges for plants

With a few exceptions, the best ph. range to get hydroponically grown plants is usually between 5.5 and 6. Lots of produce, like melons, apples, beans, squash, and berries, prefer ranging. Blueberries, alternatively, desire a much lower, more acidic ph. between 4.0 and 5.0. A fantastic idea to make use of different nutritional tanks to get plants using similar ph. ranges.

Some blossom plants have a broad optimal ph. selection. Pump kin, as an instance, will flourish in ph. between 5.5 and 7.5. Plants that need alkaline conditions contain spinach, onions, and legumes, which favors ph. levels between 6.0 and 7. Mint plants type the exact scale for an optimal ph. assortment of 7.0 to 8.0.

Average ph. ranges for nutrient systems

Hydroponic nutrient products generally focus on ph. levels between 5.5 and 6.0, the best amount for the majority of plants. The ph. range, nevertheless, is dependent upon the particular formulation. By way of instance, ammonium nitrate features a greater acidifying effect than the nitrate and also certainly will give rise to a reduction in ph. Bile salts, alternatively, create an increase in ph., leading to a more acidic solution.

Specific nourishment needs specific ph. degrees for plant uptake. The incorrect ph. amount could lead to not enough or too much of certain nutrients. As an instance, once the ph. level falls under 5.0, plants may form calcium and magnesium deficiencies or iron and aluminum toxicity. Even a ph. level above 6 or 6.5, though, could lead to iron deficiency.

Exactly why ph. degrees change from hydroponics systems

Several factors may lead to ph. amounts to shift in hydroponic techniques. After the sum of the nutrient solution falls below a toaster, the solution will become more focused while the plants consume the nourishment. This contributes to broadly varying ph. levels. It's, therefore, vital that you track nutrient therapy amounts, maintain the reservoir filled, and frequently examine the ph. from the reservoir.

Both organic and inorganic matter can affect ph. degrees in hydroponics systems. By way of instance, gravel as well as different parasitic growing media work as a buffer and lead to ph. levels to grow in media-based techniques. In a pure atmosphere, soil acts as a buffer in a related way. To acquire a precise ph. reading within a media-based system, examine the ph. of this window solution in addition to the clear answer (leachate), which drains from bags or beds which support the plants.

Algae and bacteria are the main types of organic things that affect ph. levels. If ph. ranges increase in the early and drop later in the daytime, algae could possibly be at fault. As algae absorb excess carbon dioxide through your daytime, ph. ranges increase and fall through the day. On the flip side, bacteria out of the main disorder can lead to a dramatic reduction in ph. grades. As roots decompose, bacteria will discharge acids into the hydroponic option.

The best way to keep the ideal ph. Degrees

The very first step in maintaining the ideal ph. levels is analyzing. A number of testing provides are all readily available. Evaluation strips and liquid evaluation kits will be the cheapest and accessible pool supply stores and garden centers. Digital ph. meters are more accurate and extend exceptional outcomes. You ought to examine usually with all of the hydroponic testing tools that you opt for, even daily in the event that you have recently corrected nutrient ranges or have very little experience.

Should you be using a recirculating system, then correct that the ph. degree according to evaluation results from the distribution reservoir. At a media-based system, but the ph. varies whilst the nutrient solution travels out of the source reservoir and outside throughout the rising base. Fix the ph. degrees centered on the ph. of the leachate, which drains out of the beds.

Commercially-prepared "ph. upward" and then "ph. down" services and products are readily available to keep up the ideal ph. grades. It is possible to buy these products in liquid or dry form and also utilize them in accordance with label guidelines. Ensure that you utilize services and products which are formulated for hydroponic techniques. For smaller systems or short-term outcomes, you may add weak acids like vinegar or citric acid.

Automated ph. controls cost more compared to ph. upward or ph. products down; nevertheless, they maintain the ph. at consistent levels. This method works great at recirculating systems to avoid ph. changes that occur as plants nourish.

If water is tough, the flowing effect of those elevated vitamin levels may cause elevated ph. levels. A reverse osmosis process is also an efficient and relatively very affordable way of reducing the water hardness.

Benefits of assessing and keeping ph. Degrees

Each plant requires some climbing requirements to thrive. It's worth time and attempt to track and fix the ph. degrees in hydroponic procedures. Should you understand the optimal ph. ranges to the crops, you can simply take the required measures to maintain your hydroponically-grown plants healthy?

HOW TO DESIGN YOUR OWN HYDROPONIC SYSTEM AT HOME

Measure 1: Bom - bill of materials

Parts and provides

1. Opaque container which may hold water lid (I have a vintage 18 blower storage bin)

2. Mesh pots (just how many depends upon everything you are growing along with how big is your container - I am using 6 5.25"containers) ($ 9.90 for 6 heavy-duty)

3. Rock-wool grow cube (chopped rock-wool) (5.95 for 3 liters)

4. Growing solution (I've utilized Dyna-grow brand 7-9-5 with exemplary results) ($12.95)

5. Aquarium air compressors (nothing specific) (have / not utilizing)

6. Airstone (s) along with air hose ($ 3)

7. Watch the beginning growing measure for additional schooling

Recommended but optional

1. Syringe - to creating more precise dimensions of climbing solution ($ 2.60 to get 60ml)

Construction tools

1. Razor knife

2. Pencil

3. A compass could be fine

Measure 2: produce a house for the pots

Put your strands ugly to the very top of your container lid. Now dab around each bud with a pen making certain no traces stinks.

Currently, for those who have a compass, then place it into the base radius of one's own pot. Eye-ball that the guts of each circle (or step in the event that you want) and follow the next ring in the bigger ones.

Then cut the small circle and then cut on the vertical relief cuts towards the bigger circle (view graphic for clarification). The point is always to push down the pot into the pit, and also, the container will continue closely building a far better seal.

Measure 3: aeration

My container includes breather holes at the handles, therefore that I intend on conducting my airline there. You might want to cut out a hole at the upper side or alternative site. It's not imperative at which the gap is up to it's functional. Remember, you would like to keep out sunlight out of this container and maintain out the rainwater.

Prep your atmosphere rock (s) according to the instructions about the packing (on average drinking and water soak). Please utilize new stones in order to prevent introducing contaminates.

Join your atmosphere rock (s) for an own airline and link it with an aquarium pump.

Measure 4: sterilization

Now, fill your tank. I'm assuming that your content is fresh and free from debris. Fill to the brim and add 1 tablespoon of all chlorine bleach. That is essential as it'll kill many intruders that you never need hanging out to create a problem.

Begin aeration to combine your sterilization solution - place your strands from the container too. After about 20-30 minutes, then ditch all of the water and allow the atmosphere to wash thoroughly to eradicate the chlorine.

Once this is completed, proceed to first fill and fill your own medium.

Measure 5: first load

But if you have made it this much. You are nearly done: d

Follow the directions on your nutritional supplement solution jar. My instructions involve 2 3 tsp per gallon for re-circulating approaches and one tsp / gallon to get tote systems. The main reason is nutrient toxicity (more about this later). I am going to take care of this as a tote system with only a bit more.

When filled to the appropriate degree, my container will probably soon be carrying approximately 15 gallons of drinking water. Therefore, that will require 1-5 tsp of concentrate. Shifting to ccs (the alliance in my syringe), that is about 73cc. I am going to soon be adding 80cc of attention alternative.

Thus, fill your tank with water, begin aerating, and add a suitable measured number of nutrient concentrations. Now, your garden ought to be at which you would like to buy since water is quite thick, this goes twice for bigger systems.

Measure 6: pairing plants and prepping moderate

I'll be purchasing plants that have started. I would like to develop herbaceous plants to start away since I really like having them fresh for cooking. Thus obtain plants. In the event that you'll be starting from seeds, then see the next thing.

Employing a weed, scoop out bud full of developing moderate. Squeeze somewhat, therefore put in only a tad bit more - that you never require this for clay that is fired. When you've got 6 baskets, choose 6 baskets filled with moderate and set it to a huge skillet, bowl, etc. Fill out this bowl with water and then gauge the number of gallons you've included. Afterward, step off the proper quantity of nutrient solution. Completely soak the moderate.

Even though the moderate is still soaking, wash all the dirt from the plants. Every one of them but is careful to not damage the main system. Place a bit of this expanding medium at the base of the kettle, then set the plant and then fill out the kettle along with your medium.

Set the lid on a tank, also press the pot right to an open pit. Repeat for the remainder of one's plants.

Measure 7: beginning from specified

If the final step employed for you personally, you can skip this measure - or see to your own advice;

This necessitates extra materials - chiefly rock-wool seed cubes and also a procedure to germinate. But you're likely to boil the cubes, then drop in a couple of seeds after which put on your baskets together with the conventional websites. Make certain you are able to see the cover of the seed block. Never, then put a seed to some sterile block as the sterile glass can hurt your seed (s)

You are going to need water to verify the seed receives the adoring it's needed. You might choose to set a hood on the way to produce the requirements better.

Measure 8: care

Every other week, then you have to replace your nutrient solution. Otherwise, the water will grow to be hazardous to the plant; also, it'll stunt its growth and lead to departure. Bigger surgeries do not try so since they have sufficient filtering and ways of removing toxins generated by the plants - we still do not possess this. Anyway, the plant will soak in these nutrients consequently eliminating it out of the water anyhow;

Monitor your fluid levels between water changes. When the water becomes too low, then go right ahead and top off it.

If you initially begin, you need to maintain the water level only above the bottom of the kettle. The main system will continue to work its way into the container (out from this kettle) and into the drinking water. While this occurs, lower the water level marginally (approximately an inch below the strands) and also make certain that you hold aeration going. Aeration prevents the main procedure from becoming "overly wet," and with some of this main exposed to atmosphere helps.

Measure 9: options
What else could you put in on or perform?

Well, once you're prepared - that I urge adding a water level gauge - fundamentally only a crystal clear hose which joins at the base of the container also extends perpendicular to demonstrate the most degree. This will inform you if to burn. This is going to be a prospective instruct able.

Want to develop inside? You are going to need to grow mild - that adds a considerable number of cost; however, it might be the only real solution for anyone among you in cold regions.

An easy valve positioned at the bottom of this tank can create draining simpler. In the event that you may drain into a bucket, then you may put this to use on different plants in your town.

It is a great idea to track the ph. amounts and conductivity of one's own water solution. And that I intend to visit my neighborhood pool store that really does complimentary compound testing for ph. grades. Once I've got any advice regarding the way a ph. of this water varies, I won't need to really go as usual.

Measure 10: pests

That really is a complete other instruct able, which will come soon. However, to give you a sense - you will find lots of non-invasive (even non-chemical) types of handling pests that may possibly appear.

Measure 11: lighting

I actually don't have a light strategy. I want I did; nevertheless, they might be quite costly since these have become specialized systems. Regurgitating.

What forms of lighting are all utilized for developing plants?

Most programs use hid (high-intensity discharge) lights. All of the hid methods require either ballast and bulb along with this socket and reflector. You might even make use of a t5 high definition fluorescent bulbs which combines the lighting spectrum. You are able to utilize routine t12 fluorescent bulbs to get smaller sized seedlings and cuttings.

T 5?

There are two kinds of t 5 bulbs - you for blooming plus something for the growing. In comparison for their own hid counterparts, they utilize less heat, and most of the spectrum lead is utilized by this plant. The ballast works for both kinds of bulbs.

Hid?

There are 3 chief kinds of hid: metal halide (MH), mercury vapor, and Higher Pressure Sodium (HPS). For growing, just mh and hps are all used.

What exactly do I want for hidden?

In case you are growing foliage / hairy plants (lettuce, lettuce, greens) - you need mh on a regular basis. For plants using a vegetative and blossom phase (i.e., curry, flowering annuals, fruits) - that you wish to begin with some mh and switch into hps whilst the plant blossoms and starts producing fresh fruit. If you are doing is supplementing sun lighting - utilize hps.

Imagine if I could only just afford one lighting system?

Here are some choices

1. Make use of an mh method to develop and an hps conversion bulbs for flowering.

2. Utilize hps for flowering and mh for expansion

3. Purchase a normal program and update it to an increased color corrected bulb. Most proceed for the hps system as a result of high lumen output per watt in contrast to its mh counterpart.

4. Purchase a switchable platform in which the ballast may encourage either form of bulb

5. Work with a T-5 system with trendy ceiling lamps and a hot range for flowering.

Making a straightforward wick system

1. Slice the very best in (10 cm) away from a plastic jar. Recycle a vacant 1/2 us gal (1.9 l) soda bottle. Begin your trimming using a pair of scissors or utility knife only above the jar's tag, or around 4 inches (10 cm) down from the very best. Cut around the whole bottle before the surface is wholly removed.

Employing a soft drink bottle will hold one plant. If you wish to home 10 or plants in a hydroponic garden, look at having a20 us gal (76 l) plastic bag as an alternative.

2. Poke a pit throughout the jar cap by means of a screwdriver. Put the jar cap onto a hard surface like a cutting board. Contain on the cap by its sides together with your non-dominant hand at the same time you hit a hole at the center with a palate. Make the hole roughly 1/4 in (0.64 cm) broad.

Heat the end of the screwdriver above a candle fire to melt the plastic cover in case you've got trouble hitting it.

When employing a plastic bag, use a hole saw attachment to get a hurry to create 34 holes over the center of the lid.

3. Feed a sheet of twine through the hole at the cap. Cut a slice of twin using a couple of scissors are all approximately 12 in (30 cm) long. Hold the end of the twine at the cover of the jar cap till you have approximately 6 in (15 cm) on both sides. Once the twine is via the cap, then screw it back on the jar.

When utilizing a bigger reservoir, then you might utilize a thicker bit of rope since the wick to transfer more water.

4. Fill out the floor of the jar, having a nutrient solution. Pay a visit to the community gardening store to discover a nutrient combination intended for hydroponic gardening. You are able to use exactly the exact same solution whatever you plant on the body. Fill the base of your jar with roughly 4-c (950 ml) of water. Follow the instructions in your nutrient solution to discover the sum you want to move to your own water. Once you insert the ideal amount, mix the water with a stir rod.

Use store-bought purified water on your tank in the event you've hard plain tap water.

In case you have to locate any nutritional supplement combinations from the shop, arrange a bottle on the web.

5. Place the very top of the jar upside-down and so that the twine is largely submerged. Once you have the nutrient solution mixed together, place the cover of the bottle upside together using all the

cap faces. Make certain around 1 inch (2.5 cm) of double between your jar cap and the cover of the clear answer.

When employing a plastic bag, make use of a plastic container 3--4 (7.6--10.2 cm) deep in addition to the bag lid. Be certain that you drill holes at the plastic container in order that they fall into line with all the holes in your bag.

6. Put growing moderate and also your seeds into the cover of the bottle. Search for moderate, which allows nutrients and water to readily travel, such as perlite, coconut coir, or vermiculite. Spread two handfuls of moderate in the upper section of the jar and then simmer it gently with your palms. Subsequent to the developing medium is inserted, you are able to plant your own seeds at the thickness specified in your own packaging. [6]

Each developing medium can be bought in the neighborhood gardening or yard care shop. One of these growing networking will continue to work regardless of what plants you're utilizing.

The nutrient option travels up the back in the developing moderate to supply water and food to your plants.

Wick systems operate excellent for brand new hydroponic gardeners and therefore are hands-off, nevertheless it is impossible for them to support bigger plants. Wick systems operate great for lettuce or ginseng.

Construction of a deep-water culture system

Inch. Cut a hole in the lid of a plastic java container precisely the exact same size as an internet kettle. Internet baskets have slots so that water may flow through them easily. Trace the underside of one's net pot on the coffee container lid using a pen or marker. Work with a craft knife or even a utility knife to slice the gap to size; therefore, the kettle fits snugly within the cut-out section. Keep on to shave away the sides before the rim of this web kettle is flat with the surface of the lid. [7]

A java container may take an inch plant. Should you want to generate a bigger hydroponic garden, work with a big plastic bag in the place of multiple mesh baskets.

2. Cut a little x close to the boundary of the lid to get a tube. Quantify in roughly 1/2 in (1.3 cm) in the border of the lid and then mark the place with a pencil or marker. Press on your craft knife throughout the lid to create a slit. Rotate the lid 90 degrees and also make still another slit during the one. [8]

Make your trimming just like a pit in which you place a straw in a quick food-beverage lid.

3. Feed 6 (15 cm) of air tube throughout the x. Use 1/4--1/2 at (0.64--1.27 cm) tubing on your hot water culture method. Stick at the end of the tubing throughout the x-shape you cut until it reaches on a fed at 6 (15 cm) or before the tube reaches the base of the container. Leave a tube at the top to reach a bubbler system, or just around 1 1/2 feet (46 cm). [9]

4. Fill out the java container three quarters packed with a nutrient solution. Nutrient combinations can be bought at gardening stores or on the web, and also some other combination will get the job done no matter exactly what planting is. Fill out the java container three quarters filled with tap water. Follow the instructions on the label carefully to mix the ideal quantity of nutrient liquid for that quantity of

water that you use. Make use of a stirring rod to unite the exact nutritional elements with water. Set the lid back onto your own java container. [10]

If you've got difficult tap water, then utilize bleach pressurized water on your tank alternatively.

5. Put growing seeds and medium into the internet bud. Fill out the kettle into the surface with coconut coir, perlite, or vermiculite. Sow the seeds from your own plant roughly 1⁄2 in (1.3 cm) deep on your growing medium.) [1 1]

Elect for leafy greens or greens when planting seeds rather than plants.

One of those developing mediums will operate no matter the kind of plant increased growing.

Seed thickness whilst planting might change based on the sort of plant. Talk to the seed package to determine whether they have to get implanted or deeper.

6. Attach the opposite end of the air tube into some bubbler then transform it on. Bubblers help add oxygen into the clear answer; therefore, your roots have been solved. Secure the end of your tube protruding from the cap of the container into the vent on the bubbler and then turn it on. Leave the bubbler over the entire time while the plants are still growing. [1-2]

The nutrient solution invisibly to the growing moderate on your bud, providing your plants with water and food in order that they may grow.

Deep-water nutrient programs are all reduced maintenance and simple to create in your home; however, they work nicely for plants that possess a long growing stage.

Bubblers can be bought in the neighborhood aquarium or pet shop.

Bubblers have to conduct always if not your crops may perish.

COMMON MISTAKE TO AVOID IN

HYDROPONIC

Hydroponics is a superb way to build plants at home, which is hard, fun, and very rewarding. But there is a range of issues with hydroponics which you could encounter, plus it's very important to understand how to steer clear of them or handle them successfully.

Hydroponic growth is much more specialized art than growing plants from land. It is possible to find out a lot from reading articles and books and watching videos that are educational. But, certainly, one of the greatest methods to learn is by our mistakes. Thankfully, lots of made mistakes while still growing plants using hydroponics through recent years.

Put this informative article regarding the many typical problems you might experience. Hopefully, this info will stop you from making some mistakes and provide you the data to cope with other folks.

1. Hydroponics system leaks

System flows may happen for a whole selection of explanations. Leaks can happen at any valves or join on your own body. They could also occur if your machine becomes blocked, like when the origin mass pops up an nft system, resulting in water backing up and up. Leaks may also occur in the event that you build something having a reservoir that may not hold most the nutrient solution from the computer system. Within this circumstance, a power reduction or pump failure can result in backup and over the flow of one's tank.

Solution

Examine your own body before placing any such thing. Tighten any valves and be certain all connections are secure and tight.

Assess your machine frequently for issues such as root replacements or clogged drains or sockets.

Make sure that you select a reservoir which may easily maintain most the nutrient solution from the body, not only the quantity that's inited once the machine is currently in use.

If you're using an internal system, then think about placing it onto a watertight surface, if at all possible, on a drip tray in the event that you're utilizing a little system. This really is a great concept to grab flows; however, it is going to even less clutter when tethered to its own body.

2. Buying inexpensive, insufficient or wrong lighting

I love to utilize my hydroponics systems inside; therefore, I can grow more vegetables throughout the year. Without adequate lighting of the right type, the functioning of the machine is likely to soon be very disappointing.

These created various mistakes together with indoor grow lights, like buying inexpensive lights, which were drastically wrong for exactly what I wanted or buying the incorrect form of light, which resulted in bad vegetable and fruit returns.

Solution

For many individuals, I'd strongly urge taking a look at led along with t5 fluorescent grow lights. All these are often the simplest to use, and you will be acceptable for users.

If you're purchasing led grow lights, then do not go for the most affordable option. Perform a little bit of research and buy superior lights that'll produce light at the appropriate wavelengths and at adequate amounts for the own body.

Make sure you buy enough light for the system. A fantastic guideline is to compute the square footage of this canopy of one's increasing area and multiply by 65.

Here's a fast illustration;

An increasing region of 4ft by 6ft. Complete location = 2 4 sq. ft.

24sqft x 65 = 1560 watts

With this particular growing area, you'll need approximately 1560 g of grow light. This really is a great guideline, and that's exactly what I usually adhere to.

3. Utilizing the incorrect fertilizer

When growing plants in the land, a number of the microorganism's nourishment needed to happen to be within the soil in adequate amounts. Because of this, a fertilizer developed for growing plants from dirt doesn't need to comprise lots of the follow micronutrients that are crucial for healthy plant development.

Solution

Ensure you get nutrients created for utilizing with hydroponics.

You may make your own hydroponics fertilizer out of scratch; however, it's a whole lot easier to get a several part remedy. This can become mixed to generate a nutrient solution, which can be corrected to the majority of plants and growth stages.

4. Maybe not keeping things clean

Should you allow your hydroponics installment and also the area around it turned into cluttered and dirty, you might raise the danger of spreading pests or disease into a hydroponic program.

The area of this cleanup procedure is to prevent algae, pests, and diseases from having the ability to set themselves on your process. Whilst a few individuals do conduct systems specifically made to market the development of bacteria that are beneficial, "I think for some home look-up setups, it's preferable to steer clear of pathogenic organisms, by regularly cleaning your own body and the surrounding region.

Solution

Maintain the region on your hydroponics setup clean and nicely organized.

Every 23 weeks, then drain the machine, flush the growing roots and media together with water and wash out the reservoir, tubing, and pumps.

5. Not learning as you move

Every harvest of crops at a hydroponics system differs. Some matters will probably go well, and you'll encounter several issues, either major or minor. You ought to choose the chance to test what went well, and everything went wrong to correct your clinic for plants.

Solution

Document, picture, and observe these negative and positive facets of every system you employ and harvest you grow.

If you experience an issue, start looking to get a solution. Novels, internet sites, and YouTube possess as much information available you will have the ability to address your own problems or prevent them next moment.

6. Maybe not tracking the wellness of your plants

In case you don't track your crops often, you are going to skip the first indications of issues. Whether this really is inadequate expansion or signals of lack or disorder, the sooner you realize there's an issue, the greater chance you've got of mending it and perhaps not destroying your plants.

Solution

Monitor the growth and condition of your own plants often.

If you find an issue, consider the time to learn what the issue is and attempt to improve it.

If you become aware of pests or disease, treat premature, and you also might well be able to stop excessive harm to your plants.

7. Maybe not tracking and fixing the ph. amount

The ph. level of your nutrient solution is. Probably one of the essential facets of hydroponic growing. When growing plants from land, the soil itself behaves as a ph. buffer and prevents rapid developments at the ph. level. This usually means that ph. problems are somewhat slower to grow up and also may cope with more readily.

This really isn't true for hydroponics. The ph. can alter somewhat over days or weeks because of the selection of factors including fever, speed of absorption of nourishment from the plants, presence of disorder, surplus evaporation, etc.

Solution

When developing with hydroponics, you have to track the ph. of your nutrient solution.

In a brand new system or if current modifications have been made, you might require to try to fix the ph. on an everyday basis. In a system that is stable, you're able to lessen testing to twice or once per week. Since you get to experience together with hydroponic growth, you are going to start to know that the aspects which could help determine the ph., and you'll find a sense of how frequently to try.

The ideal ph. testing alternatives would be to utilize a ph. testing lever. I generally advise obtaining an adequate quality electric ph. analyzing lever, since it generates ph. analyzing quick and simple.

8. Nutrient deficiency and toxicity

There are many factors that can trigger nutrient toxicity or deficiency in your plants. It's not always simple to tell which particular nutrient is the reason for the issue or if toxicity or deficiency would be your issue. There are many hints to watch out to find the lack and toxicity of many different nutrients, and also you are certain to receive good in pinpointing issues with experience and time.

117

Ph., temperatures, plant development rate, nutrient solution concentration, user mistake, and an entire slew of different elements can lead to nutrient issues. Remember that excess degree of one particular nutrient can result in issues with the absorption of another one.

Solution

Make sure that you compose your nutritional supplement solution carefully and accurately.

Make sure that the water you're employing to create your nutrient solution isn't overly hard. If this is so, think about diluting it with distilled water, or even using water that's experienced a reverse osmosis filter or activated carbon dioxide to decrease the degree of solids.

Monitor the focus of one's nutritional supplement solution using a ppm / EC meter

If your crops are beginning to exhibit signs of nutrient deficiency or toxicity, and my first advice will be to nourish out your body, discard the nutrient solution and also constitute a brand new batch. More capable growers might have the capability to correct matters as they proceed, but many beginners and intermediates are going to soon be better off choosing the safe strategy.

9. Employing hard-water from your hydroponics system

As stated above, using hard water may cause issues in a hydroponics system. When water remains below 200 ppm, then you're inclined to have the ability to make use of this without major issues, but regular water having a superior degree of total dissolved solids may cause problems with your nutrient solution.

Primarily, you won't have the ability to add as many nutrients into the water since you'll be restricted by your intended concentration to your nutrient answer.

Second, you're unlikely to understand the precise composition of these dissolved minerals from your tap water if you don't have experienced this independently tested.

The biggest aspects of tough water will be magnesium and calcium salts. Regrettably, these can typically be large chemical compounds, struggling to be consumed by plants.

Massive molecules of calcium chemicals in your faucet water may bring calcium salts that enhance the water, which may result in some own plants being powerless to consume these, also at the worst possible case scenario, leading to a calcium deficiency condition.

Solution

In case you have hard water higher than 200 ppm would recommend either supplementing this using distilled water or even having a filter to decrease the degree of dissolved minerals from water.

An activated carbon filter will reduce the degree of a few nutritional supplements, which also really is really a good, economical alternative.

A reverse osmosis filter can be a bit more expensive alternative but may lessen the degree of dissolved minerals near to zero.

10. Maybe not tracking ppm / EC / TDS

Employing a nutrient solution that's also dilute can result in the abrupt development of your plants. The exceptionally concentrated nutrient solution often leads to nutrient or toxicity lock outside. Neither will lead to plants that are healthy.

Since your plants absorb water and nutrients, and water can be transpired at varying speeds, and the concentration of this nutrient solution can change. The amount of change will be dependent on the development pace of your own plants, in addition to the ecological requirements of one's expanding environment.

Solution

Utilize an EC ppm TDS meter to track the nutritional supplement solution, both if creating the nutrient solution and as time passes since the plants grow.

You can adjust the answer to some level as long as the plants usually do not show some indication of nutrient deficiency or toxicity.

Change the nutrient option after having a max of 3 months. This has to be performed, whilst the proportions of the several nourishments will detract from the start concentration as a result of the factor consumed by these plants. If using regular water, then dissolved solids that must not be properly used by the plants will start to collect.

An EC meter is only going to inform you that the electric conductivity of the solution you're analyzing. That really is changed to an approximation of their sum total dissolved solids over the clear answer. It tells you about the several aspects of this solution.

Create a new batch of nutrient options every 2-3 weeks, and sooner in the event that you detect some indications of nutrient toxicity or lack on your plants.

11. Damaged or allergic pumps and taste nozzles

Hydroponics systems rely upon continuous or quite frequent delivery of nutrients and water for the plants. For those who own a nozzle or pump collapse or congestion, then these may result in issues speedily.

A busted or obstructed water pump may result in plants in many systems getting cutaway in their own water source. Wick and also dwc systems won't need this issue.

For aeroponic systems, it's quite common for spray nozzles for clogged overtime. If it comes to pass, the vulnerable roots will dry very quickly, resulting in some plants and dying quickly.

Air pumps may also neglect. It's taken also long to allow its plants to induce the quantities of dissolved oxygen from water to drop into a degree in which the roots start to float, which may end included perishing.

Solution

Assess your strategy, usually.

Look at purchasing water or air conditioner using a built-in alarm, which will sound when there's a blockage.

Look at designing your own system; therefore, if there is a congestion or collapse, it won't cause rapid plant death.

For nft technique strategies, for instance, a fantastic solution will be to leave the water socket slightly raised by the close of the station, which is going to lead to a tiny pool of water that'll stay in case of a pump failure.

12. Selecting the wrong growing moderate

The selection of increasing media is enormous, and there are lots of facets to take into consideration when building a selection. I've got still another whole article working with choosing the best climbing medium in the event that you would like for more information.

Some climbing websites are reusable; a few are really only convenient for use once. A few are absorbent and could definitely keep water across the plant roots. Some are absorbent and invite drainage. Many are expensive; some are still inexpensive. Many climbing media might be accommodated to perform in various hydroponics systems, and distinct growers are going to have their own preferences.

Solution

Have a bit of time to think about what you need your growing media todo.

Read around to find out the things other individuals have had the most success.

Consider your budget and if you need to reuse the press for multiple climbing cycles.

Read my post concerning developing media, and also you go too much wrong.

13. Maybe not flushing and refilling the device usually enough

The challenges of developing plants, together with hydroponics, are entirely worthwhile. Hydroponics has lots of advantages and can be an enjoyable hobby. But if you attempt to conduct your own body as much time between flushing out it and changing the nutrient solution, the prospect of experiencing issues, and sometimes even destroying your plants will grow somewhat. The longer you move between effects, the more inclined you should come across issues with disease, fleas, and nutrient solution problems you can't correctly treat.

Solution

While hydroponics is a lot less labor-intensive than dirt predicated gardening, it needs more frequent monitoring and modification. Flushing the device and altering the nutrient solution would be a tiny job; however, shifting is worth it. Bigger create, faster-growing plants, and all year round greens because of the kitchen will be the advantages I profit. Some simple regular maintenance of my machine will be well worth every penny, so when I gain experience, I eventually become more efficient and more true in my capacity to alter nutritional alternatives, flush out the device and wash my spare container.

14. Assembling an inconvenient hydroponics system

There are many items that may raise the hassle of a hydroponics method. Putting a machine in a little space without sufficient space to work around it, putting it somewhere your equipment isn't near hands can get bothersome. A method with a handy water source can permit one to regress the line down. A defectively developed DIY system that's likely to fail or leaks is only going to cause you frustration.

Solution

Start small. When it's a DIY strategy or even a pre-built platform, your very first few climbing cycles should really be regarded as being a learning adventure. In the event that you make bad decisions initially, you are able to proceed and plan something better time.

Plan your hydroponics system - you want to have your gear and water origin near everywhere and hand beside the machine you can make a nutrient solution or wash your equipment. If you're growing indoors, think of what could take place if there's a leak. Can it be floor watertight, or can you put a drop-down a tray.

15. Plant diseases

Hydroponic plants are usually less susceptible to infection than plants grown from dirt. With dirt, bacteria and parasites have less opportunity to prove themselves. But certain states, such as excess humidity, elevated temperatures, and too little sunlight, may greatly boost the danger of one's plants growing diseases that could endanger your whole harvest.

A variety of attributes of your own body also can cause extra stress into own plants that may cause them to become susceptible to this illness.

Solution

To stop disorder on your hydroponic plants, you ought to make an effort and prevent the conditions that germs will flourish in. This usually means avoiding too substantial temperatures and humidity ranges and seeking to make sure your plants receive some sunlight or decent quality artificial lighting.

Monitor that the ph. and attention of your nutrient solution. Make sure the nutrient solution comprises all of the necessary macro and micronutrients your plants require for growth.

Monitor your plants often for almost any indications of illness. If you notice an issue, attempt to spot the cause and cure it as speedily as you possibly can.

CPSIA information can be obtained
at www.ICGtesting.com
Printed in the USA
LVHW021027220121
677169LV00013B/452

9 781801 580281